NEW ORLEANS
SAINTS

by Brian Howell

Published by ABDO Publishing Company, 8000 West 78th Street, Edina, Minnesota 55439. Copyright © 2011 by Abdo Consulting Group, Inc. International copyrights reserved in all countries. No part of this book may be reproduced in any form without written permission from the publisher. SportsZone™ is a trademark and logo of ABDO Publishing Company.

Printed in the United States of America,
North Mankato, Minnesota
062010
092010

Editor: Chrös McDougall
Copy Editor: Nicholas Cafarelli
Interior Design and Production: Christa Schneider
Cover Design: Becky Daum

Photo Credits: Morry Gash/AP Images, cover; NFL Photos/AP Images, title page, 21, 25, 26, 29, 42 (bottom), 43 (top), 43 (middle); Paul Spinelli/AP Images, 4, 43 (bottom); David J. Phillip/AP Images, 7, 11; Mike Groll/AP Images, 8; AP Images, 12, 18, 23, 42 (middle); JRT/AP Images, 15, 42 (top); Jack Thornell/AP Images, 16; Bill Feig/AP Images, 30; James A. Finley, 33; Ben Margot, 34; Dave Martin, 36; L.G. Patterson, 38; Eric Gay, 41; John Russell, 44; Sue Ogrocki, 47

Library of Congress Cataloging-in-Publication Data
Howell, Brian, 1974-
  New Orleans Saints / Brian Howell.
    p. cm. — (Inside the NFL)
  Includes index.
  ISBN 978-1-61714-020-4
  1. New Orleans Saints (Football team)—History—Juvenile literature. I. Title.
  GV956.N366H68 2011
  796.332'640976335—dc22
                            2010017368

TABLE OF CONTENTS

CHAPTER 1

SAINTS MARCH TO THE TOP

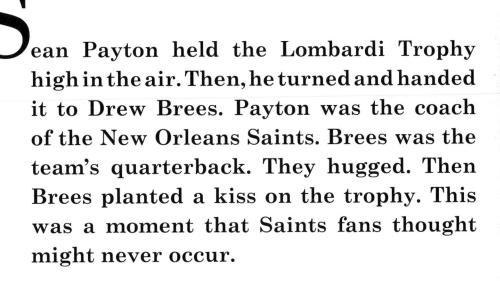

Sean Payton held the Lombardi Trophy high in the air. Then, he turned and handed it to Drew Brees. Payton was the coach of the New Orleans Saints. Brees was the team's quarterback. They hugged. Then Brees planted a kiss on the trophy. This was a moment that Saints fans thought might never occur.

On February 7, 2010, Brees and Payton led the Saints to their first Super Bowl victory. The Saints beat the Indianapolis Colts 31–17 in Super Bowl XLIV in Miami, Florida. The victory put an end to a 43-year quest to be the best in the National Football League (NFL).

GETTING THEIR CHANCE

Before the 2009 season, 27 of the NFL's 32 teams had been to the Super Bowl at least once. The Saints were one of the five teams that had never appeared in the game. After the Saints' victory in Super Bowl XLIV, just four teams remained on the list: the Cleveland Browns, the Detroit Lions, the Houston Texans, and the Jacksonville Jaguars.

QUARTERBACK DREW BREES PROUDLY LIFTS THE LOMBARDI TROPHY AFTER THE SAINTS DEFEATED THE INDIANAPOLIS COLTS IN SUPER BOWL XLIV.

COOL BREES

The 2009 season was Drew Brees's ninth in the NFL and his fourth with the Saints. He began his career by playing five seasons with the San Diego Chargers. Brees signed a six-year contract with New Orleans in 2006. He quickly picked up where he left off as one of the NFL's best quarterbacks. He threw 122 touchdown passes in his first four seasons with the Saints. Brees also made the Pro Bowl three times and was named the NFL's Offensive Player of the Year in 2008.

Brees has earned fans in New Orleans for his efforts off the field, too. After moving there, he embraced the city in a way that few professional athletes do. Brees became active in local charities. He also helped raise money to help those in need in the hurricane-battered city. Brees said the impact he has had on the city has matched the impact the city has had on him and the Saints.

"We just believed in ourselves," Brees said moments after receiving the trophy. "We knew that we had an entire city and maybe even an entire country behind us. I've tried to imagine what this moment would be like for a long time, and it's even better than expected."

Winning the Super Bowl is a major accomplishment for any football team. But the win was bigger than that for many people in New Orleans, Louisiana. The city had been devastated by Hurricane Katrina in 2005. The hurricane destroyed much of the city and many people died as a result.

The storm caused severe damage to the Saints' home

THE LOUISIANA SUPERDOME WAS SEVERELY DAMAGED BY HURRICANE KATRINA. LOCALS USED IT AS A SHELTER.

CORNERBACK TRACY PORTER CELEBRATES BY POINTING TO THE CROWD AFTER INTERCEPTING A PASS FOR A TOUCHDOWN IN SUPER BOWL XLIV.

TWO-WAY SUPPORT

"New Orleans gave us so much strength," Drew Brees said. *"The people, we knew what they had been through, and yet they continued to fight, continued to believe and continued to have faith and they helped instill that in us."*

stadium, the Louisiana Superdome. Thousands of locals had to use the stadium for shelter after their homes were destroyed. But when many people were leaving the city, the Saints stayed.

The Saints always had a strong following in New Orleans throughout their 43 mostly losing seasons. After Hurricane Katrina, that bond grew. The Saints helped bring the city together after it was torn apart by the natural disaster.

"People have asked me so many times, 'Do you look at it as a burden or extra pressure? Do you feel like you're carrying the weight of the city on your team's shoulders?'" Brees said of playing quarterback for the Saints. "I said, 'No, not at all.' We all look at it as a responsibility. Our city, our fans give us strength. We owe this to them. That's made all the difference.

"There's no city, there's no organization, there's no people that we would want to win more for than the city of New Orleans. It's an honor and just an unbelievable feeling."

Brees was voted the Most Valuable Player (MVP) of Super Bowl XLIV. He completed 32 of 39 passes for 288 yards and two touchdowns in the game. As good as Brees was that day, it was Tracy Porter who made the play Saints fans will remember.

The Saints had a 24–17 lead late in the game. But the Colts had the ball. Their quarterback, Peyton Manning, had won his

WHO DAT?

The Saints fans have had a cheer for nearly 30 years: "Who dat say dey gonna beat dem Saints?" The cheer is often shortened to simply, "Who Dat?" The origin of the phrase is unknown. But during the Saints' Super Bowl season, the team's fans and the NFL debated over who owned the phrase. The league did not want the phrase used on unofficial merchandise. Regardless, it has been a Saints tradition. In 1983, local musician Aaron Neville, a New Orleans native, and local artist Steve Monistere produced the song "Who Dat Say They Gonna Beat Dem Saints." The song also featured several Saints players.

fourth league MVP award that season. Now he was guiding the Colts down the field in search of a game-tying touchdown.

But before the Colts could reach the end zone, Manning threw an interception. Porter picked it off and ran 74 yards for a touchdown. That gave New Orleans a 31–17 lead. The Colts could not come back.

"Everything slowed down," Porter said of the play. "The spiral on the ball slowed down. The guys around me slowed down. The crowd noise stopped. It was just me and the football."

After so many years of losing seasons, the Saints were finally recognized as the best football team in the nation at the end of the 2009 season.

"We're going to enjoy this for a while," Brees said. "This is something that I think we all deserve to enjoy for a while, and reflect on what it's taken to get to this point, and all that we've been through and all that we've fought so hard to get."

SAINTS PLAYERS CARRY COACH SEAN PAYTON OFF THE FIELD IN CELEBRATION AFTER WINNING SUPER BOWL XLIV.

The NFL's expansion draft board showing Eastern Conference teams:

Cleveland Browns
Jim Battle, DE · 2 · Southern U
John Morrow, C · 11 · Michigan
Walter Roberts, Fl · 4 · San Jose St.

Dallas Cowboys
Obert Logan, DB · 3 · Trinity (Tex)
Bill Sandeman, OT · 2 · Pacific (Calif)
Larry Stephens, DT · 8 · Texas

New York Giants
Jim Garcia, DE · 3 · Purdue
Bob Scholtz, OE · 8 · Notre Dame
Gary Wood, QB · 4 · Cornell

Philadelphia Eagles
Dave Cahill, DT · 2 · Arizona State
Ray Rissmiller, OT · 2 · Georgia
Fred Whittingham, LB · 3 · Calif Poly

Pittsburg
Charlie Brad...
Jerry Simmon...
Bob Smith, 11

St. Louis Car...
Jim Heidel
Ray Ogden
Dave Simino...

Washington R...
Tom Barringto...
Don Croftcheck
Jake Kupp,

CHAPTER 2

THE NFL WELCOMES THE SAINTS

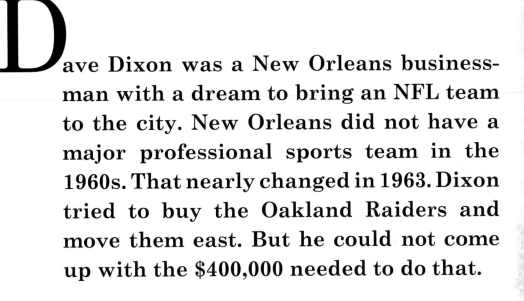

Dave Dixon was a New Orleans businessman with a dream to bring an NFL team to the city. New Orleans did not have a major professional sports team in the 1960s. That nearly changed in 1963. Dixon tried to buy the Oakland Raiders and move them east. But he could not come up with the $400,000 needed to do that.

The dream finally came true in 1966. On November 1, NFL commissioner Pete Rozelle announced that New Orleans would be given an NFL team starting in 1967. Coincidentally, that day was also the Catholic holiday All Saints' Day.

Dixon worked behind the scenes to secure the franchise. But John W. Mecom Jr. became the team owner and president. On January 9, 1967, the team was given the nickname "Saints." The name was adopted from the classic jazz song "When the

JOHN W. MECOM JR., *LEFT*, BECAME THE OWNER AND PRESIDENT WHEN THE NEW ORLEANS SAINTS BECAME AN OFFICIAL NFL TEAM.

THE FIRST SAINTS

The Saints began building their first roster right away. It started with the expansion draft on February 9, 1967. The Saints selected 42 players from the rosters of the existing NFL teams. They also selected 36 players during the 1967 American Football League (AFL)-NFL Draft. Then they made several trades to bring in veteran players. One of the last players the Saints selected during the AFL-NFL Draft was receiver Danny Abramowicz. He had a successful career and was named to the Saints Hall of Fame in 1988.

The early Saints also featured two players who would later go on to make the Pro Football Hall of Fame. The Saints traded for star defensive end Doug Atkins in 1967. He played his final three seasons for the Saints and is known as one of the best defensive ends ever. Fullback Jim Taylor only played his final season for the Saints after playing nine seasons with other teams.

Saints Go Marching In." New Orleans is widely known for its jazz music.

Fans could not wait to see the Saints. The team sold 20,000 season tickets the first day they went on sale. It sold 33,400 season tickets before the 1967 season began. Now the Saints just had to make sure they gave those fans something good to watch on the field.

The Saints worked to build a winning team before the 1967 season. That included making two big trades. Those trades brought in quarterback Gary Cuozzo and fullback Jim Taylor.

Cuozzo had spent four years as a backup to future Hall of Fame quarterback Johnny Unitas with the Baltimore Colts. But he had done well when he did play. Taylor

SAINTS RUNNING BACK DON MCCALL ROUNDS THE CORNER DURING A GAME AGAINST THE CLEVELAND BROWNS IN 1967.

was considered the NFL's best fullback. With those two leading the way, the Saints were hopeful for a good first season.

The Saints won their last five preseason games. They

HOME FIELD

The Saints played their home games at Tulane Stadium on the Tulane University campus. That was their home through the 1974 season. In 1975, the Louisiana Superdome opened and the Saints began playing there.

JOHN GILLIAM RETURNS THE OPENING KICKOFF 94 YARDS DURING THE SAINTS' FIRST REGULAR SEASON GAME IN 1967.

hoped to take that success into the regular season. New Orleans played its first official game on September 17, 1967. The team faced the Los Angeles Rams at Tulane Stadium. More than 80,000 fans were on hand for that game. Their excitement could not be contained. That was especially true when Taylor was introduced. He was a native of nearby Baton Rouge, Louisiana, and a former Louisiana State University star.

Said linebacker Steve Stonebreaker, "The roar that greeted

him was unbelievable and unforgettable. Then came Gilliam's flight. That was a miracle."

Stonebreaker was referring to John Gilliam. The rookie receiver wasted no time making Saints history. On the opening kickoff against the Rams—the very first play of the Saints' first official game—Gilliam ran 94 yards for a touchdown. Despite that thrilling start, the Saints lost to the Rams 27–13.

The Saints had a talented team. But they had a tough task ahead. Expansion teams had never done very well in their first seasons. It turned out the Saints were no different. They lost their first seven games and finished 3–11 in 1967.

Life did not get any easier after that. Taylor retired after just one season with the Saints. Cuozzo also demanded

WHAT A THRILL

John Gilliam scored a touchdown on the first play in Saints history when he returned a kickoff 94 yards for a touchdown on September 17, 1967. "I was a rookie, nervous and afraid," he said. " The football was kicked down the middle, and I prayed to the Lord, 'Please go to the Flea [teammate Walt Roberts],' but Roberts called it for me. I caught it and took off running to save my hide. I ran behind a wedge of blockers and went past them about midfield. I veered to my left, and I was running free. What a great feeling. What a super feeling!"

to be traded after that first season. The Saints went 4–9–1 in 1968. They got a little better in 1969. They finished 5–9 but still had a long way to go. The fans remained loyal even with the struggles. They filled Tulane Stadium every week. Coach Tom Fears looked to the future with hope.

"They are real tough competitors," he said of his players. "I've never seen this group quit."

CHAPTER 3

TOUGH TIMES

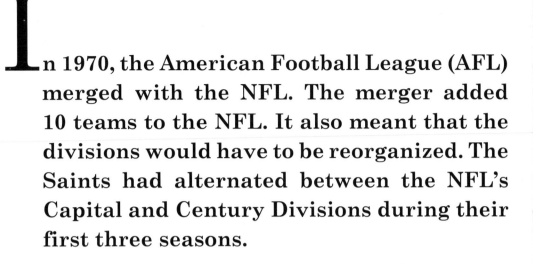

In 1970, the American Football League (AFL) merged with the NFL. The merger added 10 teams to the NFL. It also meant that the divisions would have to be reorganized. The Saints had alternated between the NFL's Capital and Century Divisions during their first three seasons.

They had been paired with the Dallas Cowboys, the Philadelphia Eagles, and the Washington Redskins in the Capital Division in 1967 and 1969. The Saints spent the 1968 season in the Century Division with the Cleveland Browns, the St. Louis Cardinals, and the Pittsburgh Steelers. In 1970, they moved to the National Football Conference (NFC) West division. Joining them in the division were the Atlanta Falcons, the Los Angeles Rams, and the San Francisco 49ers.

Changing divisions did not change the fortunes of the Saints. After winning five games in 1969, the Saints won just twice in 1970. They finished 2–11–1. The team fired coach

TOM DEMPSEY KICKS A 63-YARD FIELD GOAL AGAINST THE DETROIT LIONS IN 1970. IT WAS STILL AN NFL RECORD THROUGH 2009.

DEMPSEY'S KICK

The 1970 season was one of the worst in Saints history. But it did have one signature moment. The Saints were hosting the Detroit Lions on November 8 at Tulane Stadium. Detroit was leading 17–16 as time wound down. On the last play of the game, Saints kicker Tom Dempsey nailed a 63-yard field goal to secure a 19–17 win. It was the longest field goal in NFL history. "I saw the ref with his hands up in the air, and I heard the crowd, and I had to accept the fact that I'd done it," Dempsey said.

Dempsey was born without toes on his right foot. That forced him to wear a special shoe on his kicking foot. Still, Dempsey played 11 NFL seasons. His 63-yard kick to beat the Lions still stands as the longest in NFL history through 2009. The Denver Broncos' Jason Elam tied the record on October 25, 1998. Dempsey only played in New Orleans for the 1969 and 1970 seasons. However, he is a member of the team's Hall of Fame.

Tom Fears after going 1–5–1 during the first half of the season. Fears had been the team's coach since its first season. He was replaced by J. D. Roberts. Roberts would coach the Saints through the 1972 season.

As much as they tried, the Saints could never find a winning formula during the 1970s. They drafted quarterback Archie Manning with the second pick in the 1971 NFL Draft. Although Manning had become one of the league's top quarterbacks, the Saints continued to struggle. They had a losing record every year until 1979. Even then they only finished 8–8. The league had switched to a 16-game season in 1978.

DESPITE DRAFTING STANDOUT QUARTERBACK ARCHIE MANNING IN 1970, THE SAINTS HAD A LOSING RECORD EVERY YEAR UNTIL 1979.

THE FIRST GREAT MANNING

Archie Manning was the number two pick in the 1971 NFL Draft by the New Orleans Saints. Years later, two of his sons would become first picks in the draft. Peyton Manning was taken first by the Indianapolis Colts in 1998. Eli Manning was taken first overall by the San Diego Chargers in 2004. However, Eli was immediately traded to the New York Giants.

Both Peyton and Eli would go on to win a Super Bowl. Archie was not as lucky. The Saints never had a winning season when he was there. But he was twice selected to the Pro Bowl. He also holds the Saints' all-time record for passing yards. He was one of the first two players named to the Saints Hall of Fame in 1988. The other player was wide receiver Danny Abramowicz. On the Saints' fortieth anniversary, Archie was named to their all-time team.

The Saints had six different head coaches throughout the 1970s. One of them was future Hall of Fame coach Hank Stram. But even he could not help the Saints. The team finished 7–21 during his two seasons with the club in 1976 and 1977.

Manning was a native of nearby Mississippi. He never lost hope. "Ever since last season ended," Manning said after the 1980 season, "the number one question people ask me is, 'Why don't you leave? Why don't you get out of here?' It's kind of hard to explain. I've put in 10 years here, this team, this city. Sure I want to win, but I want to win here, in this city."

The fans had to find things other than winning to get excited about in the 1970s. They had one of those moments in 1975. The Saints moved out

IN 1975, THE SAINTS MOVED INTO THEIR NEW STADIUM, THE LOUISIANA SUPERDOME, WHICH COULD SEAT 69,056 FANS.

of Tulane Stadium after eight years there. They moved into the brand-new Louisiana Superdome. The Saints did not have a winning football team, but they had great fan support. After 1975, they had what was considered the best stadium in pro football. The Superdome seated 69,056 fans.

SUPER STADIUM

The Louisiana Superdome cost $163 million to build. The city of New Orleans lost a lot of money on the stadium in its early years. But it has become one of the great sports stadiums in the United States. The Superdome has hosted six Super Bowls, more than any other stadium. It has also been the home to college football's Sugar Bowl, major boxing matches, the college basketball Final Four several times, music concerts, and national conventions.

The 1970s were disappointing for most Saints fans. The 1980s did not get off to a much better start. The Saints lost their first 14 games of the 1980 season. Coach Dick Nolan was fired after the twelfth loss. The Saints finished 1–15 that season.

Manning was traded to the Houston Oilers one game into the 1982 season. But the Saints showed signs of improvement in the following years. They matched a team record with eight wins in 1983 and nearly made the playoffs. The Saints needed a win against the Los Angeles Rams in the last game of the regular season to get in. But they ended up losing on a last-second field goal.

The Saints then went back to losing records. They won only seven games in 1984 and 1986. They won only five in 1985. By the end of the 1986 season, the Saints had played 20 seasons in the NFL. Yet they had never had a winning record and had never been to the playoffs.

"We were the league's doormats," said Derland Moore, a Saints defensive lineman from 1973 to 1985. "When I went out and people would ask me if I played for the Saints, I would say no."

The fans craved a winner. Manning could only imagine what the city would be like if the Saints were to host a playoff

GAME PREPARATION

NFL Films followed the Saints throughout one week of the 1976 season for the film Six Days to Sunday. The crew filmed everything as the team prepared to play the Green Bay Packers. That included practices and team meetings. Coach Hank Stram was fired after the 1977 season, however. The film was never shown. Bringing back some of the old footage, NFL Films finally aired the show in 2001—25 years after it was filmed.

SAINTS TACKLE DAVE LAFARY TRIES TO STOP LOS ANGELES RAIDERS HALL OF FAME DEFENSIVE END HOWIE LONG DURING A 1985 LOSS.

game. In 1981, he said, "Can you imagine what our place, the Superdome, would be like if we were ever a winner, if we had a playoff game here? They'd blow the lid right off the place. Nothing could hold a candle to it."

Manning was long gone by 1986. But the Saints were about to find out what it was like.

CHAPTER 4
LEARNING TO WIN

The Saints had been around for 20 years. Yet the team still had not experienced a winning season or a playoff game. Nine men had served as head coach during that time. All nine of them failed to win. The tenth coach was Jim Mora. He took over for the 1986 season. It did not take long for him to do what the others could not.

SAINTS FOR SALE

John W. Mecom Jr. owned the Saints from the beginning of the team. In 1985, he put them up for sale. Some fans feared that a new owner would move the Saints out of New Orleans. Local car dealer Tom Benson put an end to those fears. He purchased the Saints for about $70 million. Benson has remained the owner of the Saints through 2010.

Mora's first Saints team finished 7–9. But they laid the foundation for a decade of winning like Saints fans had never seen before.

By late in the 1986 season, the Saints began grabbing attention around the NFL for their

WIDE RECEIVER ERIC MARTIN CATCHES A PASS IN THE END ZONE DURING A GAME AGAINST THE MINNESOTA VIKINGS IN 1987.

work on the field. They were 6–5 through 11 games and were in the race for a playoff spot. "We're better than people perceived us to be," Saints general manager Jim Finks said at the time. "All in all, I'd say we're making progress."

The Saints went 1–4 the rest of the way. But progress had been made. The Saints would make a giant leap forward in 1987.

Louisiana native Bobby Hebert established himself as the starting quarterback that year. With Hebert and Mora, the Saints had their best season to date in 1987. The season was shortened from 16 to 15 games that season due to a players' strike. Three of those games were played by replacement players.

The regular players played in the first two games of the season before striking. After a week of no football, the replacements played three games.

The Saints were 3–2 at the end of the strike. They went 9–1 after that and finished 12–3. The Saints made the playoffs for the first time. "The big difference is the attitude of the players; it's a reflection of Jim Mora," said

MORA'S IMPACT

When Jim Mora was hired by the Saints in 1986, he knew how to win, but the Saints did not. From 1983 to 1985, Mora coached the Philadelphia/Baltimore Stars of the United States Football League (USFL). The Stars went 48–13–1 under Mora and played in all three USFL championship games, winning two of them. He then led the Saints to the first four playoff appearances in team history and compiled a 93–74 record with them. After his time in New Orleans, he coached the Indianapolis Colts for four seasons, guiding them to the playoffs twice.

QUARTERBACK BOBBY HEBERT TURNS TO HAND OFF THE BALL DURING A GAME AGAINST THE LOS ANGELES RAMS IN 1989.

LINEBACKER PAT SWILLING (56), THE 1991 NFL DEFENSIVE MVP, CELEBRATES AFTER TACKLING A MINNESOTA VIKINGS' PLAYER IN 1991.

Archie Manning. He was a radio broadcaster for the Saints in 1987.

The playoffs did not bring glory, however. New Orleans lost to the Minnesota Vikings 44–10 at the Superdome. Even with the loss, the 1987 season was a turning point for the Saints. The team made the playoffs four times in Mora's first seven seasons as coach. That included three straight years from 1990 to 1992. They also won their first division title in 1991. They went 11–5 to win the NFC West.

Mora's time as coach ended on a sour note during his eleventh season. He resigned after a 2–6 start to the 1996 season. It was a tough day for Mora and the Saints when he resigned. But he had changed the team. "I hope everyone will remember that this team never had a winning season until he became our coach," owner Tom Benson said on the day Mora resigned.

The Saints hired Hall of Fame player Mike Ditka to coach the team after the dis-appointing 1996 season. Ditka had led the Chicago Bears to the Super Bowl XX title after the 1985 season. But he never could re-energize the Saints. New Orleans was 15–33 in his three seasons as coach.

THE DOME PATROL

During the late 1980s and early 1990s, the Saints featured one of the best sets of linebackers the NFL has ever seen. They were known as the Dome Patrol. The group included a mix of Rickey Jackson, Vaughan Johnson, Sam Mills, and Pat Swilling over the years. The Dome Patrol helped New Orleans have its first winning season and playoff appear-ance in 1987.

From 1983 until 1991, the four players combined to have 18 Pro Bowl selections. All four played together from 1986 until 1992. Swilling was named the NFL's Defensive Player of the Year in 1991. Jackson, however, was the biggest star. In 2010, he became the first player who played most of his career with the Saints to be enshrined in the Pro Football Hall of Fame. During 13 years with the Saints, he amassed 115 sacks and seven interceptions. Sacks were not recorded during his rookie season.

Ditka was fired after the 1999 season. Jim Haslett replaced him. Haslett guided the Saints to a 10–6 record in 2000. It was their first playoff appearance since 1992. The Saints also won their second NFC West championship.

The Saints had another first before the season was over: they won a playoff game. New Orleans took a 31–7 fourth-quarter lead against the St. Louis Rams. But the defending Super Bowl champion Rams began a comeback. The Saints held on to win 31–28 at the Superdome. Wide receiver Willie Jackson had 142 receiving yards and three touchdowns to lead the Saints that day.

"You could hear a lot of people out there saying, 'Same old Saints,'" Benson said after watching his team give up almost all of its 24-point lead. "But we did it. We held on."

The Saints lost to the Vikings to end their season one week later. But they had reached a new milestone for the club. It would not last, however. Haslett failed to lead the Saints to the playoffs in any of the next five seasons.

ONE OF THE GREATS

William Roaf never caught or threw a pass and he never scored a touchdown. But he was one of the best Saints of all time—and one of the greatest offensive tackles in NFL history. The 6-foot-5, 305-pound tackle was the Saints' first-round draft pick in 1993. Roaf started at tackle for them every year from 1993 to 2001. He played in seven consecutive Pro Bowls from 1994 to 2000. Roaf was also named first-team All-Pro twice. "The best I've ever been around," Saints assistant coach Paul Boudreau said early in Roaf's career. "He could be the best tackle ever."

QUARTERBACK AARON BROOKS LOOKS DOWNFIELD FOR AN OPEN RECEIVER DURING A GAME AGAINST THE ST. LOUIS RAMS IN 2000.

CHAPTER 5

FROM TRAGEDY TO TRIUMPH

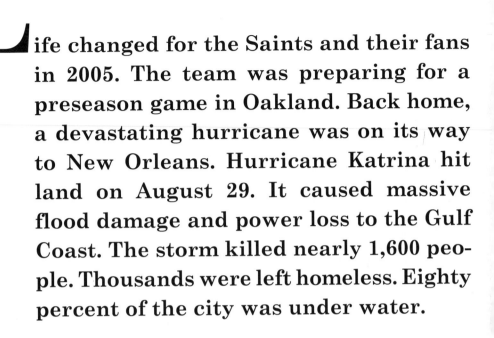

Life changed for the Saints and their fans in 2005. The team was preparing for a preseason game in Oakland. Back home, a devastating hurricane was on its way to New Orleans. Hurricane Katrina hit land on August 29. It caused massive flood damage and power loss to the Gulf Coast. The storm killed nearly 1,600 people. Thousands were left homeless. Eighty percent of the city was under water.

The Saints' home was also damaged. There was a hole in the roof of the Superdome. Still, the stadium became a shelter for thousands of displaced residents.

The city began its long road to recovery. The Saints did, too.

But they still had to play the 2005 season. The Saints played a pre-season game in Oakland three days after the hurricane. When it was over, they were unable to go back to New Orleans. Instead they flew to San Antonio, Texas. They would operate from

MEMBERS OF THE NEW ORLEANS SAINTS BOW THEIR HEADS DURING A MOMENT OF SILENCE FOR HURRICANE KATRINA VICTIMS IN 2005.

IN 2006, THE SAINTS ACQUIRED QUARTERBACK DREW BREES, *RIGHT*, AND DRAFTED RUNNING BACK REGGIE BUSH, *LEFT*, TO IMPROVE THE OFFENSE.

SOMETHING MORE

Before 2005, the Saints were like any other team. Their main goal was to play well and win games. After Hurricane Katrina struck New Orleans in 2005, some players felt a new motivation. "We're playing for everybody who experienced loss and tragedy during the hurricane," running back Fred McAfee said. "If we can show people that hope is real, we'll be doing our part."

San Antonio for the rest of the 2005 season.

The Saints played "home" games in New Jersey, San Antonio, and Baton Rouge, Louisiana, during the 2005 season. Three games were at the Alamodome in San Antonio. Four were at

Tiger Stadium in Baton Rouge, home of Louisiana State University. The Saints' "home opener" was played against the New York Giants in the Giants' home stadium in New Jersey.

It was difficult for the Saints to focus on football. But the team knew that their fans needed them. "Right now the team is their lifeline, their connection to what was real—because what they're experiencing is surreal," running back Fred McAfee said of the fans.

The Saints went into 2005 with playoff hopes. They won their first game in dramatic fashion. John Carney kicked a last-second field goal for a 23–20 win over the Carolina Panthers. It was one of few highlights for the Saints on the field, however. They finished 3–13 and won just once in their last 12 games.

"Everybody on this team is on the same page now—to do everything we can to help the survivors, and to play for each other as a team," wide receiver Joe Horn said. "Football ain't nothin' compared to somebody who lost a loved one or who doesn't have a house to go back to, but we feel them and they feel us, and we're representing a region that's resilient."

The Saints went through several changes after that season. Coach Jim Haslett was fired and replaced by Sean Payton. The team also signed quarterback Drew Brees. He had

HOMETOWN HEROES

Shortly after Hurricane Katrina, several Saints players visited the ravaged city. Among them were running back Deuce McAllister and wide receiver Joe Horn. As they visited the city, they realized what the Saints meant to the victims. "Don't worry, we're gonna represent Louisiana," Horn told one man.

been a star with the San Diego Chargers. The Saints selected running back Reggie Bush in the first round of the 2006 NFL Draft. He had won the Heisman Trophy as college football's best player. All three changes would make a significant impact on the future of the Saints.

Some people worried that the Saints would permanently relocate after Hurricane Katrina. But the team returned to the Superdome in 2006. The Saints went 10–6 and won the NFC South division that season. They defeated the Philadelphia Eagles 27–24 in the playoffs. It was the team's second-ever playoff win.

The Saints then played in their first NFC Championship Game. The magic ended there.

They lost to the Chicago Bears 39–14. The Saints went a combined 15–17 during the next two seasons but then rose to new heights in 2009.

The Saints started 13–0 in 2009. They finished the regular season 13–3 and with the best record in the NFC. That earned them a bye in the first round of the playoffs. They beat the Arizona Cardinals 45–14 in the second round. Then they hosted the Minnesota Vikings in the NFC Championship Game.

LOSING A LEGEND

Linebacker Sam Mills was one of the best players in Saints history. He played for them from 1986 to 1994. In April 2005, Mills passed away after a battle with cancer. "Nobody worked as hard as he did. A great man, a great friend," said Chuck Commiskey, who played with Mills in New Orleans and also in the upstart USFL.

SAINTS RUNNING BACK REGGIE BUSH LEAPS OVER A ST. LOUIS RAMS' DEFENDER AND INTO THE END ZONE DURING A 2009 GAME.

New Orleans and Minnesota had been the dominant teams in the NFC all season. The Saints came out on top when they finally met. They won 31–28 in overtime to earn their first trip to the Super Bowl.

The Saints had been tremendous in the regular season. But many people still favored the Indianapolis Colts in Super Bowl XLIV. The Colts had started the season 14–0, but they lost their final two games as many of their star players rested. The Colts came out strong and jumped to a 10–0 lead in Super Bowl XLIV. But two touchdown passes by Brees helped the Saints come back and take a 24–17 lead in the fourth quarter. Moments later, Saints cornerback Tracy Porter returned an interception 74 yards for a touchdown that wrapped up the Saints' 31–17 victory.

New Orleans is a city known for its partying on Mardi Gras. The Saints gave them another reason to party in February 2010. The fans had stuck by the team during years of losing. After Hurricane Katrina, the Saints stuck with New Orleans and helped the residents stay positive during challenging times.

The Saints knew that winning the Super Bowl was not just about one game. It was about bringing pride to a team and a city that had suffered long enough.

"You play this game to try to be the best and you play to win

BREAKTHROUGH

Before the 2009 season, the Saints had played in eight playoff games. They had won just two of them. In 2009, the Saints went 3–0 in the playoffs. Coach Sean Payton has led the Saints to a 4–1 record in the playoffs.

NEW ORLEANS SAINTS FANS HOLD UP SIGNS TO CELEBRATE THEIR
TEAM'S 31–17 SUPER BOWL XLIV VICTORY OVER THE INDIANAPOLIS COLTS.

the ultimate prize," Brees said after the Super Bowl. "You think of all those that came before, not only the teams and the coaches, but the players and those that paved the way for all of us to be able to play this great game that we do. This is something that can never be taken away from you, and as long as we live, even beyond our lifetime, our kids' lifetime, our grandkids' lifetime, this is something that will always be with us. It will be part of our legacy and that's special."

TIMELINE

1966	On November 1, the NFL announces that New Orleans will be home to the league's sixteenth team. On December 27, Tom Fears is named the first head coach.
1967	The team is named the Saints on January 9. The roster begins to take shape through the expansion draft, the NFL Draft, trades, and free-agent signings.
1967	The Saints play their first regular-season game on September 17, losing to the Los Angeles Rams 27–13. On November 5, they record their first win, 31–24 over the Philadelphia Eagles.
1970	Saints kicker Tom Dempsey kicks an NFL-record 63-yard field goal on the last play of the game to defeat the Detroit Lions 19–17 on November 8.
1971	On January 28, the Saints draft Mississippi quarterback Archie Manning with the number two pick in the NFL Draft.
1975	The Louisiana Superdome opens.
1985	On May 31, New Orleans businessman Tom Benson buys the Saints from John W. Mecom Jr. for $70 million.
1986	Jim Mora is named the tenth head coach in Saints history on January 28. He would coach the team for 10 plus years and lead them to their first four playoff appearances.
1987	The Saints qualify for the playoffs for the first time in team history. They finish the season with a team-record 12 wins. In the playoffs, the Saints lose to the Minnesota Vikings, 44–10, at the Superdome.

1991	The Saints finish 11–5 and win the NFC West division for the first time.
1992	The Saints qualify for the playoffs for the third straight year. Once again, they cannot break through in the playoffs, losing to the Philadelphia Eagles 36–20 in the first round.
2000	Jim Haslett is named the team's head coach in February. That season, he leads the Saints to a 10–6 record and their second division championship. The Saints also win a playoff game for the first time, 31–28, against the St. Louis Rams.
2005	Hurricane Katrina hits New Orleans in August, bringing massive destruction to the city. The Saints move their headquarters to San Antonio, Texas, for the season and play their home games in three different stadiums.
2006	On January 18, Sean Payton is named the fourteenth head coach in team history and on March 14, the Saints sign free-agent quarterback Drew Brees. After a 10–6 season, the Saints advance to the NFC Championship Game for the first time.
2009	Enjoying the best season in team history, the Saints start 13–0 and finish 13–3. In the playoffs, they defeat the Arizona Cardinals and the Minnesota Vikings to reach the Super Bowl.
2010	At Super Bowl XLIV, the Saints defeat the Indianapolis Colts 31–17 on February 7.

QUICK STATS

FRANCHISE HISTORY

1967–

SUPER BOWLS
(wins in bold)

2009 (XLIV)

NFC CHAMPIONSHIP GAMES
(since 1970 AFL-NFL merger)

2006, 2009

DIVISION CHAMPIONSHIPS
(since 1970 AFL-NFL merger)

1991, 2000, 2006, 2009

KEY PLAYERS
(position, seasons with team)

Morten Andersen (K, 1982–94)
Drew Brees (QB, 2006–)
Hoby Brenner (TE, 1981–93)
Stan Brock (T, 1980–92)
Bobby Hebert (QB; 1985–89,
    1991–92)
Dalton Hilliard (RB, 1986–93)
Joe Horn (WR, 2000–06)
Rickey Jackson (LB, 1981–93)
Vaughan Johnson (LB, 1986–93)
Archie Manning (QB, 1971–82)
Eric Martin (WR, 1985–93)
Deuce McAllister (RB, 2001–09)
Sam Mills (LB, 1986–94)
Derland Moore (DT, 1973–85)
William Roaf (T, 1993–2001)
George Rogers (RB, 1981–84)
Pat Swilling (LB, 1986–92)

KEY COACHES

Jim Mora (1986–96): 93–74;
    0–4 (playoffs)
Sean Payton (2006–): 38–26;
    4–1 (playoffs)

HOME FIELDS

Louisiana Superdome (1975–)
Tulane Stadium (1967–1974)

* All statistics through 2009 season

QUOTES AND ANECDOTES

Bobby Hebert was the first quarterback to lead the Saints to the playoffs. It was fitting that he was the one to do it. Hebert was born in Cut Off, Louisiana, located about 65 miles (105 km) south of New Orleans. He starred at Northwestern State University in Natchitoches, Louisiana. He joined the Saints in 1985 and led them to the playoffs three times.

The United States Football League (USFL) wasn't around very long—just from 1983 to 1985. But it helped develop some of the best players and coaches in Saints history. Jim Mora, who won more games than any other coach for the Saints, came to New Orleans from the USFL. Quarterback Bobby Hebert and linebackers Vaughan Johnson and Sam Mills also starred in the USFL before coming to the Saints. Cornerback Antonio Gibson and running back Buford Jordan were among several other Saints who came from the USFL.

In 1999, Saints head coach Mike Ditka pulled off a huge trade. He traded eight draft picks to the Washington Redskins to get rookie running back Ricky Williams. Williams had won college football's Heisman Trophy in 1998. The trade did not work as planned. Williams had an injury-filled rookie season, and the Saints finished 3–13, leading to Ditka being fired. Williams played just three seasons with the Saints.

The Heisman Trophy is awarded every year to the top player in college football. Five Heisman Trophy winners have played for the Saints. They are running backs Reggie Bush, Earl Campbell, George Rogers, and Ricky Williams, and quarterback Danny Wuerffel. In addition, 1956 Heisman winner Paul Hornung was selected by the Saints in the 1967 expansion draft and participated in training camp, but he retired before the season and never played for the Saints.

GLOSSARY

burden

An obligation that is difficult.

emerge

To become noticed.

expansion

In sports, adding a franchise or franchises to a league.

franchise

An entire sports organization, including the players, coaches, and staff.

hall of fame

A place built to honor noteworthy achievements by athletes in their respective sports.

Heisman Trophy

An award given to the top college football player each year.

merge

To unite into a single body.

ravage

To damage.

replacement players

Players brought in while others are on strike.

resilient

Recovering from adversity.

strike

A work stoppage by employees in protest of working conditions.

surreal

Something that seems to be unreal or like a dream.

tradition

Something that is handed down.

FOR MORE INFORMATION

Further Reading

Donnes, Alan. *Patron Saints*. New York: Center Street, 2007.

Fathow, Dan. *The New Orleans Saints Story*. New Orleans, LA.: Megalodon Entertainment LLC, 2010.

Marching In: The World Champion New Orleans Saints. Chicago: Triumph Books, 2010.

Web Links

To learn more about the New Orleans Saints, visit ABDO Publishing Company online at **www.abdopublishing.com**. Web sites about the Saints are featured on our Book Links page. These links are routinely monitored and updated to provide the most current information available.

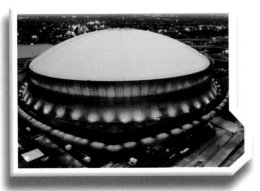

Places to Visit

Louisiana Superdome
Sugar Bowl Drive
New Orleans, LA 70112
504-587-3663 or 800-756-7074
www.superdome.com
The Saints play their home exhibition, regular-season, and playoff games here.

New Orleans Saints Hall of Fame Museum
415 Williams Blvd.
Kenner, LA 70062
504-471-2154
www.neworleanssaints.com/team/history/hall-of-fame.html
This museum is home to exhibits and memorabilia representing the history of the New Orleans Saints. The museum is open free of charge to season ticket holders, and it is open on game days.

Pro Football Hall of Fame
2121 George Halas Drive Northwest
Canton, OH 44708
330-456-8207
www.profootballhof.com
This hall of fame and museum highlights the greatest players and moments in the history of the National Football League. Six people affiliated with the Saints are enshrined, including Rickey Jackson and Jim Finks.

INDEX

About the Author

Brian Howell is a freelance writer based in Denver, Colorado. He has been a sports journalist for more than 17 years, writing about high school and college athletics, as well as major events such as the U.S. Open golf tournament, the World Series, and the Stanley Cup playoffs. He now covers the Denver Broncos for the *Longmont Times-Call*. He has earned several writing awards during his career. A native of Colorado, he lives with his wife and four children in Colorado.